Contents

Personal Growth and Development

TIME BOUND

SETTING YOUR GOALS

MONIQUE JOINER SIEDLAK

Oshun
Publications

Cover Design by MJS

Cover Image by ikostudio@depositphotos.com

Published by Oshun Publications

www.oshunpublications.com

Other Books in Series

Personal and Self Development
Creative Visualization
Astral Projection for Beginners
Meditation for Beginners
Reiki for Beginners
Manifesting With the Law of Attraction
Stress Management

Want to learn about African Magic, Wicca, or even Reiki while cleaning your home, exercising, or driving to work? I know it's tough these days to simply find the time to relax and curl up with a good book. This is why I'm delighted to share that I have books available in audiobook format.

Best of all, you can get the audiobook version of this book or any other book by me for free as part of a 30-day Audible trial.

Members get free audiobooks every month and exclusive discounts. It's an excellent way to explore and determine if audiobook learning works for you.

If you're not satisfied, you can cancel anytime within the trial period. You won't be charged, and you can still keep your book. To choose your free audiobook, visit:

WANT TO BE FIRST TO KNOW?!

JOIN MY NEWSLETTER!
MOJOSIEDLAK.COM/SELF-HELP-AND-YOGA-NEWSLETTER

Introduction

One of the most unfortunate things I have seen over time and have discovered is that there are so many users that have learned to develop the things called "Time Management and Goal Setting" but for some unknown reason or lack of fore-sight they have chosen not to use this habit- skill in all the possible areas of their lives.

So my challenge to you today after reading this is if you are that person or individual who is only allowing yourself to permit these techniques to permeate only limited areas of your life, why not now take a strong look toward translating these things we call time Management and Goal Setting into greater areas of your life, and to do it with one keyword in mind, "Balance."

Goals can be in the right person's hands a wonderful tool. A key to helping an individual generate the combination of both emotions and physical actionable undertakings to meet that one's desired expectations in life or for others a mirror of discontent and pain if you could not follow through. But please learn how to always remember that with goals, they can always be changed to fit your current circumstances as no one goal fits all, your goal is yours and it is up to you to make it work and fit for you.

That's why it is so important that you first understand the importance and need to learn the fine art of mastering how to put in the time necessary towards brainstorming your goals and objectives in life, and to learn to cultivate and build up this habitual way of thinking into the beginning and middle of all your medium to long-term goal setting as it will help you keep on track to make the changes needed to reach your desired need.

After you have chosen what will be your main goal, it will then be time well spent testing that this goal of yours is the real deal for you. For this chosen goal to stand any chance of ever achieving it, and wanting to take action now!

ONE

The Importance of Setting Goals

Almost all the great business people or individuals, who have been successful in their fields, have applied this important method in their lives. It is about creating specific goals with the determined commitment to fulfill them.

What appears to mind when you think about goals? Surely they will be great plans for your life, as you look from here to several years, get those great desires you have longed for a long time and work so that one day you can fulfill your dreams. All of these seem long-term goals and many times these are what drive us and make us dream. But let me tell you that the most important goals and those that will make you improve day after day, are the short-term goals.

The Short-Term Goals

These are important because they are what will help us be grounded. They are what teach us the importance of hard work. Although it is true, setting goals is done with the future in mind, but you never forget that the basis of your future will be molded according to the present you are building. To reach the big goals, you must first meet some smaller ones, because there are no shortcuts in the way of success.

Setting daily goals and not so difficult ones to achieve is a good challenge you can put yourself, do it in your work, do it in your business, set goals of your bills to pay in the short term, do it in your home. Promise yourself to accomplish those goals, organize yourself and write them to remember them. You will see how building in your present position to advance more and grow in an unforeseen way. Each day will be a step on the right path, the path of your great goal.

If one of your most prized goals is to graduate from your school studies in the career you are studying, an excellent illustration of short-term goals would be to get a good grade in a specific project. Perhaps to attend all classes every day missing none.

These are daily goals you can perform. They are not impossible; they simply require your effort and determination. Another goal and a very important one in terms of the goal of finishing your higher studies, maybe you organize your time and determine two times daily to study, whether you have pending tasks or nor. This habit will make you very disciplined and as a result, you will get your long-term goal in a less complicated and safe way.

Many times we won't be able to meet our goals. There is the disappointment and discouragement when we elaborate our goals and realize that we are not able to achieve them. Many people surrender at first, but this happens because we do not see the true problem.

Before setting your goals, it is important that you study your abilities. Do not go too far from a single step if your legs are not long enough. Set realistic goals, which can be overcome. Little by little, you can increase those goals, but the first thing you must experience is the satisfaction of having committed to something and then finish it. This feeling will be the force that drives you to go for more. The illusion is a key element to fulfill your dreams, so do not despair. Walk at your pace, but never stop or veer. The important thing is that you go ahead with a winning attitude!

TWO

Setting Goals for Personal Development

PERSONAL DEVELOPMENT GOALS ARE THE PATH YOU CAN choose to move your life forward. The means to attaining those goals is to set them.

Decide Your Personal Development Goals

You will need to make a few choices. Just like the decision that is carried out when creating a business plan, your personal business plan will involve work.

Your research on your personal business plan will be to sit down and figure out your own priorities. Look at your lifestyle as it is now. Whatever makes you happy, search for ways to expand that. Whatever makes you unhappy or causes you to stress, search for ways to adjust that for the better.

The areas that most people will look at are professional, social, spiritual, family, neighborhood, etc.

Write Your Personal Development Goals/ Personal Business Plan

Write your personal development goals. This isn't actually as simple as creating a list, but it is a comprehensive examination of what you need and how you will get there.

My Personal Development Goals: Career

Because the least personal of these are professional options, let's use that as an example.

I want to use my life as an illustration of how to put these two steps together. I had a job I disliked. Greatly. I didn't want to go to work, was irritable with my family when I got home and felt like I was spinning my wheels.

The first step in my personal business plan was to figure out where I wanted. Simple, I want a six-figure income with a reasonable expectation of the security.

Now, how to get there. Working for someone else is out of the question, so I was looking at ways to make that money. One aspect of what I did was to go back to writing. As a writer and publisher, I produce a quality product. With self-publishing on the rise, this was the perfect way to go.

Next, I figured out what it would take for me to make the money I wanted doing what I chose. I planned each day with that end goal in mind and looked at the path I needed to travel to get there.

Finally, I wrote it down. Not just "I want a six-figure income from writing," but a plan that looked something like this.

I will start my writing career on December 1st.

I will make X amount of dollars in my first year.

To do this, I will write every day.

I will find new ways to distribute my books.

The key is that I didn't sit down and write. I set my personal development goals down, with a clear path. My personal development goals became my personal business plan. That plan guided every minute of the day.

My Personal Business Plan

By identifying the goal in the distance and outlining a direction, your personal development goals will turn into your personal business plan.

This is identical to deciding to drive out of state. I decide where I am going. I plot a course, avoiding as much traffic and construction as possible. If I encounter an obstacle, an accident or even debris on the road, I go around it. I have the route memorized and the end goal is still in my sights.

Personal Development Goals Road Trip

Accomplishing your personal development goals needs to be no more complicated than planning a trip to a new location. First, decide where you're going. How you will get there. Last, take reasonable precautions against difficulties and concerns.

A Constitution, Not the Ten Commandments

It does not mean this to be a rigid, unchanging set of inflexible rules. Your personal business plan will be a living, breathing document that will change as you change. It will need to adapt to the world around you and your changing personal development goals.

A Word of Encouragement

Start today with your personal development goals. Pick one aspect of your life, make a few decisions and then write your personal business plan. Even if you only figure out what you want to do for your health, it's a giant step forward.

It's all up to you. You decide. That's why we call them your personal development goals.

THREE

Setting Goals Increases Self Esteem

WITH OVERCOMING OBSTACLES OR REACHING GOALS, possessing good self-esteem can make a difference. Self-esteem is based on the concepts you have about yourself, your judgments of your skills, emotions, and actions. In this way, you conform to a personal image that is perceived as "self-image."

An individual with positive self-esteem is one who has a clear attitude towards herself. She knows what her qualities are and what her weaknesses are and she feels safe and happy with her own way of being.

This self-image forms from your childhood and is formed to reach adulthood. The issue of having a negative or altered self-image is that you yourself can bring about the "stones of the road," that is, placing obstacles to your personal achievement and your happiness.

People who have low self-esteem are habitually too critical, perfectionist and self-blaming. Having a negative thinking style, it torments them all day long with messages like "you're stupid," "you're useless," "you're a failure," "this is too good to happen to you." Negative thinking and blaming also paralyzes you, because it does not give you the opportunity to try or accept the prospect of failing or making mistakes.

How to Identify If You Have Low Self-Esteem

The individual with low self-esteem normally:

Doubt constantly about their actions

Feel he has nothing to share

He does not like expressing his opinions or intentions for dread of rejection

Feels self-conscious in a scene of social contact

Seek confirmation of others

Recognizes others as stronger, smarter or more attractive

Sees other individuals as superior to himself

She chastises herself for her mistakes and failures

Decreases its value or its achievements

Envy's others

He feels guilty

He feels unattractive

If you share some of these traits, it is very important that you work on your self-esteem today. Follow these tips:

Silence the Inner Negative Voice

That voice that is accusing and tormenting you all day can change. Maybe you have not thought about it, but that voice is not you. Not all your personality is that voice. Face it and try to separate it from your other thoughts. For example, if he says "you're a failure, it always goes badly for you," You must say to yourself in response, "no, I am not a failure. Sometimes I do well and sometimes I do badly. This time I did not have a good result, but next time I will be much better prepared."

Catch Negative Thoughts

Become an observer of your thoughts. Whenever a negative thought arises, immediately change it to a positive one. You can take a notebook to write these ideas and replace them in writing. This will allow you to see the issues you worry the most and make you feel bad. It can prepare you to change them when they assault you during the day.

Involve yourself in some activity that makes you feel fantastic

We all have qualities, virtues, and gifts. There must be something that deeply passions you and what you are fantastic at. Dedicate yourself to that and do it with great joy, without thinking whether it is right or wrong, only in order to enjoy and feel valuable.

Don't Compare Yourself

There is a phrase that says, "The grass is always greener." This means we usually see other people's lives better than ours. We observe only the achievements and not the difficulties or mistakes of others and we feel bad because we do not have the same. That is envy. No one is in anyone's shoes, so the ideal is that you have your own goals and that you compete with yourself and not with the imaginary life of another person.

Be Self-Pitying

Self-pitying is a mental embrace you create yourself and with which you deal with yourself completely. If you stop to think about your negative thinking, maybe you would understand that you would never tell another person the terrible things you say. It's time to be self-pitying. Think you are to treat well that person with whom you live every minute of your life, yes, with yourself. Say positive and beautiful things. Give yourself encouragement and learn to forgive your mistakes.

I hope these tips will help you have a happier and fuller life. You are a valuable and unique person.

FOUR

Setting Goals Changes Your Reality

Change

CHANGE YOUR LIFE, CHANGE YOUR JOB, HAVE MORE FREE TIME, change your bank account! Who has not declared one day to wish to change situations? So often after a flashy start, many returns to square one to never to leave there. It's these people try to change the wrong way, how does not work.

Here are two ideas to change:

Refuse the reality and try to change it.

Believe the reality and change it.

This is an important paradox. We have to acknowledge what we want to change so we can change it. You cannot change a situation you refuse or reject to look at because it causes you to feel uncomfortable. Once this is determined, you will need to establish three groups of intentions to change, for example, significantly, sustainably and for the best.

Change What You Get

Recognition of the demand for change develops from there. You know you dislike the results you get. Logically you adjust them. But for that, it is vital that with this aim there is a clear target so you can reach it. It must tempt enough to inspire you and you believe it is achievable. Otherwise, you will act boldly for a while, then you will come back to the beginning, you will give up.

But once this is set up, you cannot be satisfied with just that. You cannot concentrate on the results. It will work for the simplest things, but not for the most interesting ones. You will need to achieve this goal of a new result.

Change Behaviors

It is essential to set goals that will be steps and actions to get what you want. If you want to increase your turnover by 40%, you will sooner or later have to draw up plans, develop strategies and act according to this strategy. In other areas, it seems even more obvious. If you want to build muscle or lose weight, you will do new things, eat differently, play sports, charge more a bar for training, etc.

Anyone who has changed their habits may find adopting new behaviors may be uncomfortable. It is often a challenge. Wanting to change a behavior without considering another dimension of change is doomed to failure.

Who You Are

Your identity will condition your thoughts, emotions, and actions. Your personality is often something quite arbitrary. It is more of a presence you have on yourself than a reality. By cons, this looks conscious or unconscious condition your reality and your limits.

Ask yourself this question to accept change. What type of person do I have to become to live what I want to live? If you want exceptional results, think exceptionally. It will allow you exceptional emotions that will condition exceptional actions.

I will tell you a secret. No one ever realizes a defeat. People realize what is consistent with their identity. The real feat would to become a world champion without training and having no talent, is not it? It's impossible. It is more logical for the champion to achieve the exceptional than not to do it because it is his identity. And this identity conditions the rest. Besides, what happens when he loses the connection to his identity as a winner? He stops winning. He then has results consistent with his new identity.

FIVE

Setting Goals Is Good

NOW YOU ARE CLEAR YOU WISH TO LOSE WEIGHT, YOU MUST set an obtainable goal to reach it. It is not about losing weight fast, simply lose weight. That has specific intentions.

In this experience, food will play a key part. When we think about health and nutrition, we assume of salads and water glasses, but for that, there are the professionals who are not merely teachers who will instruct us how to lose weight fast but offer a proper diet for our special target.

One of the most essential steps is to recognize we are not alone on this path. There is a whole field of research compiled for years by individuals who battle against overweight.

The initial action is to determine what we want. Do we do it for health? To avoid diabetes? To have a better appearance? Or all the above?

Once we have it, we're on the way.

When you show up to your specialist and he sees you already have this in advance, both will save a lot of time to take these three steps.

Step One: Change Outcome Goals to Habit Purpose

These represent what we will do and not what we get that will determine everything. It is not the same as saying, "I will lose ten pounds" or "I will stop consuming sugary drinks."

We talk about reality and this is the greatest example. In the past, there have been consultants who presented a model picture to their patients and informed them, "This could be you." And never took place to be.

The dream starts with the work. Working for daily goals is the only path to achieve them. That is why the transformation of habits is more significant than the desire itself.

The goal of habits is the process you will show your commitment to yourself.

Step Two: Change Prohibition to Concentration

Prohibiting almost guarantees you will. It is a natural resistance to shift and we will all go through it. It is ineffective when they say no to you; it's when you have the most concern to do it.

This is where we must change prohibiting concentrating. In this way, we will take the mind to where it should be away from temptations and distractions.

Concentration with objectives focuses on the feeling of well-being. Look for easy actions that work for you and repeat them. For example, to attack hunger you eat a piece of fruit. Your response would never leave home without fruit and consult with your doctor the quantities and which you can ingest so it does not impact your established diet.

Step Three: Change Performance to A Circle of Influence

Performance targets are more identified with external recognition. As children, we hoped for the little star on our forehead the teacher gave us more than learning. We were not interested in getting something of the task, but the simple little star.

The goal of a more favorable domain would have been to concentrate on taking advantage of the activity they left us. It would reflect which in a good job and eventually there would be a star on the forehead.

This is the way to lose weight. We should concentrate more on the well-being of our body than on the flattering comment, "Are you losing weight? How good you look."

SIX

How to Set Goals

REGARDLESS OF WHETHER YOU HAVE SMALL DREAMS OR HIGH intentions, setting goals allows you to plan how you wish to lead your life. Some achievements can take a lifetime while some can be achieved during the course a day. You can set big goals or plan specific manageable goals. In both instances, you will have a sense of success and self-worth. The onset may look overwhelming, but you will learn how to work steadily until you reach even the most ambitious dream.

Set Goals You Can Reach

Ask yourself some crucial questions about what you want in life. What do you want to achieve today, within a year and throughout your life? The answers to these questions can be as general as, "I want to be happy," or "I want to help people." Look at what you want to get in 10 or 15 years from now.

A professional goal in your life could be to open your own business. A goal connected to your physical state could be to be in excellent shape. A personal goal could be to have a family and home one day. These can be huge goals.

Divide the overall goal into smaller and more specific goals

Consider the areas of your life you want to change or you think you would like to develop. The areas could include your career, your finances, your family, your education or your wealth. Ask yourself questions about what you would like to achieve in each area and how you would like to approach it in five years.

For a goal in life, you could want to be in decent shape. Set a smaller goal of running a marathon or eating healthier meals.

For a goal in life like starting a business of your own, you could set smaller goals such as learning to take care of business effectively and how to open a clothing store.

Write Short-Term Goals

Now you have a concept of what you wish to accomplish in a few years, form concrete goals for you to work on them now. Set a deadline within a sensible amount of time but only a year for short-term goals.

Writing your goals will make it tougher to overlook them, which will make you responsible for them.

To be in good shape, your first goals may be to eat more fruits and vegetables and run a 5k marathon.

To open your own business, your first goal may be to take an accounting class and find the perfect location for your clothing store.

Make the goal steps that will move you to your goals in life.

Basically, you must decide why you are setting this goal and what you will get with it. Some useful questions you can ask yourself when you figure this out are: do you think it's worth it? Is this the appropriate time for it? Does this match my needs?

For example, a short-term goal connected to your physical condition might be to practice a new sport within six months.

However, ask yourself if this will help you achieve your larger goal of running a marathon. If the answer is no, consider changing your short-term goal for something that will help you be one step closer to fulfilling your goal in life.

Adapt Your Goals Periodically

You are likely to put measures in place to achieve your great goals in life, but take time to reevaluate your smaller goals. Are you reaching them according to the set time period? Are they still necessary to reach your biggest life goals? You can be flexible and adapt your goals.

To be in good shape, it is possible that you will have to master the 5k races. After running in some races and struggling to overcome your personal best times, you may have to adapt your goal and change it from running a 5k race to running a 10k race. Over time, you can change it to running a half marathon and then to running a marathon.

To open your own business, after you have completed the first goals of taking an accounting class and finding a location, you will probably have to set new goals to get a business loan to get the space and ask the local administration or government for the license for your business. Next, you can get or rent the space. Find the books to you need, select and hire the staff. Now you're ready to open the doors of the business to the public. Over time, you could even decide to open a second store.

SEVEN

Practice Effective Strategies

Make Your Goals Specific

WHEN YOU SET GOALS, THEY MUST ANSWER SPECIFIC questions: who what, when, where, and why. For every specific goal you set, you must ask yourself why it is a goal and in what manner it is helpful for your goals in life.

To open your own business, you should create a short-term goal of taking an accounting class. This can answer the questions: Who? Myself. What? Take an accounting class. Where? In the library or accounting class somewhere. When? Every Saturday for twelve weeks. Why? To learn how to manage an account for my business.

To be in good shape, which is general, you should create a specific goal "run a marathon," which starts with the short-term goal of running a 5k race. When you look at each of the short-term goals, you can answer these questions: Who? Myself. What? Run a 5k race. Where? Downtown. When? In six weeks. Why? To be closer to my goal of running a marathon.

Create Measurable Goals

To record our progress, the goals must be quantifiable. I will walk more is a much harder goal to record and measure than; I will walk around the track about sixteen times every day. Basically, you will need a way to determine if you are reaching your goal.

Running a 5k race is a measurable goal. You will know with certainty if you fulfill it. It is likely that you will have to set a goal even in the short term such as run at least one mile three times a week to achieve your first 5k race. After you're your first 5k race, a measured goal would be to run another 5k race in a month, but reduce my time by four minutes.

A measurable goal would be taking an accounting class. It is a specific class in which you will sign up to attend every week. A less measurable alternative would be to learn to account, which is vague. It is tricky to know when you have completed the learning of accounting with this tactic.

Are Your Goals Practical?

It is important to analyze your situation honestly. Recognize which goals are reasonable and which are unlikely. Ask yourself if you have everything you need to reach your goals such as skills, resources, time, and knowledge.

If you want to open your own clothing store, but do not have the background in taking care of a business, you do not have the cash or finance to open the business and you do not know how clothing stores work or you are not interested in reading, you apparently will not reach your goals.

To be in good shape to compete in a marathon, you must spend a lot of time running. If you do not have sufficient time or enthusiasm to spend many hours a week, this goal may not work for you. If this is your case, you could adapt your goals.

There are other ways in which you can be in good shape and that do not require you hours of running.

Check Priorities

At a specific time, you will have a sum of goals, all in various stages of execution. Deciding which goals are more significant or with less time is essential. If you have too many goals, you will get overwhelmed and less prone to meet them.

It may be useful to choose some major priorities. This will allow you to focus on whether a conflict between goals arises. If you have to choose between completing one or two secondary goals and completing one of the primary priorities, you must choose the leading priority.

If you are struggling to be in good shape and have set smaller goals such as eating healthier foods, running a 5k race and swimming a mile three days a week, you will probably recognize that you do not have the time or stamina to do all those actions at one time. You can prioritize. If you wish to run a marathon, running a 5k race first may be more important to your goal than swimming every week. You can continue to eat healthier since, in addition to helping you run, it is also good for your overall health.

If you are struggling to open your own clothing store, you will probably need to get a business license or permit and make certain you qualify for a business loan, if you need it, before you start choosing the specific books that you will have in your store.

Keep a Record of Your Progress

Writing a journal is an excellent way to keep track of your personal and professional progress. Analyzing yourself and realizing the progress made to reach a particular goal is essential to keep you motivated. This can even inspire you to try harder.

Asking a friend to help you stay on track can keep you focused. For example, if you are training for an important career, meeting a friend frequently and exercising together can keep you on track for your progress.

If you are exercising to participate in a marathon, keep a jogging journal diary in which you record how long you can run, how long it took and how you felt. As you get better and better, this can be great to improve your confidence and to check it and see how much you have improved since you started.

Recording your progress in relation to opening your own business can be slightly more challenging, but write down all your secondary goals and then cross them out or indicate if they have been completed can help you keep track of the work you have done.

Evaluate Your Goals

Recognize when you have reached your goals and celebrate it accordingly. Take this time to evaluate the process of the goal, from its conception to its completion. Consider whether the time span or your skills made you happy or if the goal was feasible.

For example, after running your first 5k race thank yourself that you were able to finish a goal, even if it seems insignificant compared to your biggest goal of running a marathon.

It is obvious that you will celebrate when you open the doors of your clothing store and make your first sale to a customer since you will know that you successfully strived to reach your goal.

Keep Fixing Goals

After having reached the goals, even the most important ones in life, you will want to keep growing and setting new goals.

After running the marathon, you should evaluate what you would like to do next. Do you want to run another marathon, but improve your time? Do you want to vary and try a triathlon or an Ironman? Or do you want to race again for short distances like 5k or 10k?

EIGHT

Three Surefire Steps to Take Charge of Your Goals

WELL, YOU KNOW TO ACHIEVE INCREDIBLE RESULTS, TO BE successful in your life, start from believing you can do it, set goals and establish plans and taking action. With none of the above-mentioned steps, it is impossible you will achieve what you want.

Nine out of ten people who set their goal fail to achieve what they want. Does this mean that goal setting is not working? What about the one person that makes his or her dreams comes true? In fact, it is not that goal setting does not work, it is just that people are getting excited, and they set their goals and only take a little action for a few days.

After that, they lose the drive that keeps them going. They somehow procrastinate and stop taking any action anymore. That is why most individuals did not achieve what they want even if they have set their goals.

Now, before you set your goals, there are three guaranteed ways you must follow to stay motivated all the time. Many people start their goals but give up as soon as they started. This is because they did not follow these three keys that will supercharge them toward their goals.

Set Specific and Clear Goals

Yes, I believe you know about this. If you will set goals, your goals must be clear and specific. The more specific your goals, the easier you can frame your mind to achieve it. It will create such an intense image in your mind that propels you into taking action right away.

So the first thing about your goals is that they must be clear and specific. Becoming rich is not clear, however, to make the $1000. In two months will be clear. Therefore, make sure you know what you want, be specific.

Set the Deadline

Once you have your goals set, you need to know when you will achieve it. Without a deadline, your mind will not create a sense of urgency, and that's why you will not achieve it.

Once you have a deadline for your goals, your mind will tell you it is time to achieve it. It will somehow force you into taking action. Think about it, whether you are in school or in your work, you will get your work done whenever the deadline is near.

Set Stretch Goals

What are stretch goals? Stretch goals are the goals that are excited and are challenging. To earn $1000 in your business is not a stretch goal. It is an incremental goal. This is because you can simply achieve it by working harder. While for stretch goals, it is something like earning $50,000 in your business.

A stretch goal will force your mind to operate from a creative mind frame. You know if you keep on doing the same thing, putting more effort and time, it is possible for you to achieve your incremental goals like earning an extra $200. However, for stretch goals, they are not the same. You will not achieve it if you are using the same approach. Working harder and spending more time will not earn you an extra $50,000.

This is how your mind will force you into taking new creative actions, coming up with new strategies to achieve your exciting goals.

Remember, if you are going to set your goals today, make sure you follow all the three steps mentioned here.

NINE

The Importance of Setting Deadlines for Your Goals

PEOPLE TEND TO EXTEND THEIR TASKS, TO OCCUPY THE TIME we have planned for its success. If we hold two hours in our schedule for a meeting, that meeting will take us precisely those two hours and if we set aside an hour, we will be able to carry it out in just one hour.

Our mind guides us to try to fulfill the time we set ourselves in the fulfillment of things. For this reason, when we set a deadline for a specific task, our mind forces us to fulfill our responsibility and prepares our body to complete the task one way or another, conforming to the time we have set. Our body chemically reacts unconsciously, preparing for the pattern of activity we need to finish the task successfully.

For this reason, it is essential to set deadlines for our priority goals, because if we do, we predispose our mind and body to accomplish the task when it must be finished. Without a deadline, goals are often postponed day after day due to procrastination.

In addition, a psychological effect occurs when setting a deadline, when the time is coming, we develop concentration, raise enthusiasm and experience a greater ability to do things. Seeing that the final hour is approaching drives us to make a final effort that implies a great increase in efficiency and productivity. It's like when the runner is reaching the end of the race and makes a great final effort to make the best time. Without a goal line, the runner would never do that sprint.

The deadline represents a challenge, which drives us to express our capacity and productivity. Because it is a challenge which forces us to use our full potential for success. By meeting the deadlines, we find satisfaction and motivation and become a commitment to ourselves, we become able to materialize our goals and turn our dreams into reality.

Setting deadlines is an effective way to manage time to be more productive. Establishing deadlines helps us to say no to interruptions and time criminals and to stop providing self-excuses to ourselves so as not to face the reality that the absence of protection of time is to our disadvantage.

TEN

Finding Time to Achieve Your Goals

FINDING TIME TO ACHIEVE YOUR GOALS IS ROUTINELY A challenge. Whether you are single, married, have a family, work a part-time job or full-time job, there are always projects, tasks, and individuals that will demand your time. If your goals are not significant enough, it is easy to let them slide, and let your ordinary life take over. If you wish to avoid this and turn your dreams into reality, then follow the tips below.

Deadline

Setting a deadline for your goals would have to be the most powerful step in reaching them. Deadlines are wonderful things. When you have one at work, you pull out all the stops to achieve it. You find yourself more motivated and more productive. You need to harness this power in your goal setting. Set up a definite end date for your big goals and clear end dates for each task. Once you set these, work towards them. Allow yourself some down time adequate breaks so you feel refreshed.

Plan Your Day

Allocate your time into slots and work on your goals and only on your goals during this time. Free yourself from distractions, even take the phone off the hook and work towards your success. It doesn't have to be a large amount of time. Even half an hour each day will progress you to your achievements at lightning speed.

Know why you want to achieve them. If your goals are important enough to you and you can see the benefits of reaching them, then you will find time for them. Put your goals in a place you can see them every day and place memorabilia on your desk, at home or in your car to remind you why they are so important.

Get others on board. If your family is on board, then it will be easier to find time for your goals. Ask them for half an hour each day and share with them the benefits. Don't juggle the kids and your goals at the same time. This won't work well and will increase your stress levels and your kids.

Make a Public Commitment

Make a commitment to a friend or a mentor about when you will complete your goals. This will motivate you to work on your goals.

Each of us has the same amount of minutes in an hour, hours in a day and days in a week. What is different is how we use this time. If you place your goals as a high priority on your daily to-do list, and your goals are important to you, then you will find time to work on them every day.

ELEVEN

Sharing Your Goals

NEVER UNDERESTIMATE THE CAPABILITY OF MUTUAL SUPPORT to help you reach your goals.

Declaring a goal, sketching out a plan and taking necessary actions to carry out our dreams can be a solitary business. We usually plan alone and, work alone and frequently even celebrate our success alone, by choice, but when we involve a goal buddy in our dreams, our efforts can be massively enriched. Here's why:

Enhanced Belief

The right individual to share your goal is the person who believes in you. It might be someone you love who wants the best for you, but not always. Often, wishing the best for you will involve advising you against your plans, because you might fail. It is protective behavior, but it doesn't help.

Often the best goal buddy is someone who is less involved, but who sees something in you they can believe in. When they do, they reinforce your own belief. Whether your supporter is next door or halfway around the world, their faith will spur you on when you need it most.

Daily Encouragement

The effort of daily action when our spirits are low and progress seems elusive can sometimes feel impossible. Having a keen and sympathetic supporter makes all the difference. An encouraging phone call, a shared cup of coffee or just a brief e-mail reminding you of your aims and that they are there for you will be a huge pick me up faced with gloom.

Stable Outlook

We all know the old saying about not seeing the wood for the trees. Well, if you work alone, it is all too easy to see things from the wrong perspective, to put too much emphasis on some things and too little on others, without realizing it.

A goal buddy will give you a more balanced view, an outsider's perspective. They will often pot out things that should be blindingly obvious but which you have missed due to your intense focus. A good supporter will be your touch-stone to reality.

Ideas and Advice

No matter how clever and creative you are, you will never think of everything. An effective goal buddy will offer you new ideas. Suggest new angles and ask new and searching questions to inspire your creativity even further.

They do not have to be authorities in your field, but if they have intelligence and imagination, they will bring their own unique skills to your niche and together you will create something unique.

The Extended System

The final bonus that your goal buddy brings is the chance to reach a wider circle of buddies. As well as enjoying what your buddy knows, you can enjoy who they know.

You may struggle with particularly thorny obstacles in your path and out of the blue, your buddy says, "I know a guy who can do that," and you're on your way again. Suddenly you have access to skills, information, and expertise from a far bigger network than you ever thought possible.

So why not look at your goals? See how much you could enjoy a good goal buddy.

TWELVE

Accountability Partner and Mastermind Group

OFTEN BUSINESS OWNERS GET STUCK IN THE DETAILS OF running their business and lose track of the big picture. A Mastermind group can offer support and feedback from other entrepreneurs who know you and your business well, to help you see how and where you are getting stuck. I've been to a number of mastermind groups over the years and continue with a couple because they are worth more than the time and effort. If you are a solo-entrepreneur or running a small closely held business without an outside advisor or board of directors. A Mastermind group of peers in different businesses or even within your profession can be invaluable.

A good group will help you evaluate opportunities, guide you to resources and provide accountability. They should support you in growing your business, help you keep moving through the hard places/phases, and brainstorm ideas for new opportunities, solving problems and attracting more clients. It allows you to work on your business instead of in your business, examine other viewpoints and main your vision. In addition, you benefit from the creative ideas of many people instead of just your own limited thoughts.

The Mastermind can help solve your biggest challenges,

get you out of your comfort zone delving into new opportunities and hold you accountable so that you're more likely to take action and reach your goals. If you want to create your own Mastermind, here are some tips to get you started.

The first step is to get clear on what you want to create. The clearer, more specific (think numbers and dates) you are on your vision and the outcomes you want, the more likely you are to achieve them.

What's your business' mission? How do you define success? What do you want your business (and life) to look like in one, three, five years? Must have: written goals and objectives. Less than five percent of people write out their goals, but those who do are much more likely to achieve them than those who don't. They must be:

Specific

Not I want to earn a lot of money, but I want to earn $XXX,XXX per week/month/year.

Measurable $XXX,XXX by this date, short, medium, and long-term.

Believable

Six-figure incomes and million dollar bank accounts are fine but what do you really believe you can accomplish in the next few years?

Now you're ready to form your Mastermind group. Who or at least what type of people do you want on your team? Think about who you know how you'd like to invite. Would be the right partners for you? Common wisdom holds that you're as (or will be as) successful as the five people you spend the most time with. Your income and success tend to be in the same range as the group you're connected with so choose wisely and be careful in selecting people for your Mastermind. You want to be selective. It's always simpler to add individuals to the Mastermind later and quality over quantity is integral.

An effective business Mastermind usually involves four to ten individuals, but it can differ depending on the rules your group set up. You need to depend on the people you work with. Confidentiality is the most significant part of Mastermind groups. To clients, prospects, and competitors, you need your business to look respectable, but in a Mastermind group, you can admit to the glitches, the failures and challenges without being penalized because everything discussed stays in the group.

There are a number of ways to locate compatible members. It's imperative you interview people before you accept them to the group. Look for individuals that display certain qualities. For example, you want to make certain you have individuals that are taking action types and not negative victim type.

You need people eager to improve. This is an excellent moment to be brave. Contact the director of the Chamber of Commerce, local networking groups, other civic organizations you belong to. Explain what you're doing and that you're seeking like-minded people to join you. You'll be pleasantly surprised at the feedback. If they can't join you, they'll know of others who'd like to. You can always place ads, online forums, and social networking sites if you'll be teleconferencing, and social associations (school, church, charitable groups) to discover more potential members. Know what you require to get out of being a part of a Mastermind. What would be the best conclusion you could accomplish? If these individuals were your board of directors, how would you prefer to connect with them?

Establish protocols for trust, honesty, confidentiality, responsibility, timeless and accountability. Groups can meet weekly, monthly or quarterly in person or via teleconferences or some combination. Once you have found a few core members, survey them and decide what everyone brings to the table and what additional skill sets would be a good addition. Most groups usually want to vote unanimously on new members once a Mastermind is established, too, which is fair considering how detailed people can get when revealing business secrets. Agendas can be set or they can allow each member an amount of time. You also need to decide when and where to meet, and if you want to have a leader or if you want to rotate leadership. Somebody needs to be accountable for watching time, relaying messages if people miss a meeting and contacting people if there's a change.

Decide how long each meeting should last. This would include for face-to-face meetings, socializing and break time. Figure out how long each member gets to talk.

It is important to stick to this schedule, or people get frustrated because meeting run too long and there isn't a clear focus. Consider collecting dues. The funds can go to paying for meeting space, refreshments or social activities. Paying a small monthly fee keeps the commitment level higher and establishes the importance of the Mastermind in members' business plans. When you make all of these decisions and it's time for your first meeting, remember to set and agree to the rules and goals from the start. Number one rule is that everything said during the meeting needs to be confidential.

Other rules may include prohibitions on shooting down ideas, reminding members to maintain an open mind, not be absent or late too frequently. Decide on consequences for the rule violations. How will absences be handled? If the group is small, they may set meetings to accommodate members' changing schedules.

Be consistent though. It requires regular attendance for all members to gain the greatest benefit of the Mastermind. Everybody should also identify a long-term goal on the first meeting. Encourage people to share brain food such as books, music, movies, quotations, websites, software, and so on. Identifying areas of expertise and experience will add dimension to the relationships. Make sure you set a timer as each person talks, carefully making sure that everybody talks only as long as they have set for them. When people give feedback, it needs to be brief and to the point so that everybody can give feedback according to time allotments. Sometimes feedback won't be needed, a person might decide to simply ask to be held accountable for something by the next meeting, ask if anybody needs accountability until the next meeting. They may require a call from another member to keep them in focus.

In future meetings, make sure that everybody gives a brief update of their progress from the last meeting. Review rules periodically so that everyone follows them. The biggest problem frequently is people talking past their allotted time span. It's excellent for each member to get a chance to take an authority position. One individual, periodically rotating, may host the meeting reminds people of the day and time, sets the tone, promotes the conversation and manages the pace so that everyone gets air time. Or, you may assign roles to each member: meeting scheduler, host, note taker, and timekeeper. As Napoleon Hill discovered so many years ago and detailed in the classic Think Rich and Grow Rich, the Mastermind is a dynamic component of success. Masterminds help keep you stimulated and excited about your projects.

How often have you started a new project, get excited about it and later quickly lost focus? The support and accountability of a Mastermind group can help you remain on course. If you tell the group you will accomplish something by next meeting and you don't do it, you'll hear about it. You know what they say about peer pressure? It works. It might be work in the beginning, but a well-organized and designed Mastermind group is more than worth the effort. Take action, create your own Mastermind group, and see your goals emerge.

THIRTEEN

Ways to Practically Apply the Principle of Pareto

Do you know the Pareto Law? You may have read something about it, or even apply it day by day. However, now we will look at a good way to implement it in our personal lives to maximize our productivity and increase our results. The Pareto Law says 20% of the effort generates 80% of the results.

Pareto (which is the name of the person who applied for this law) determined with experiments that this law applies to lots of situations in real life and that most times it may not be 20% or 80% accurate. It could be 23% and 79%, which these values are around 20 and 80.

The most interesting of all is the number of situations in which it relates as we will learn below. Learning how to take advantage of this law can bring us great benefits and cut down our efforts.

The Pareto principle has many important consequences for our everyday life that can produce a strong benefit if we employ them.

Mastering a Subject

By learning something if we invest 20% of the effort we can get 80% of the result. Take any matter. Getting to master it is laborious. But to become perfect (or relatively perfect) in it is even more difficult. So think if really in that matter compensates all that dedicated effort.

Reading Nonfiction

I can devote 100% of my time to reading a book that is very interesting. Or I can dedicate 20% of my time to each of the five books, which I will get to know 80%. With this, I will achieve a much more efficient result.

Working with Clients

The customer is always right; they say. But 20% of the clients that produce 80% of the benefit have even more reason than the others. These are the customers you cannot screw up with.

Growing Income

It is also possible that 20% of your effort produces 80% of the benefit. Maybe it makes little sense for you to dedicate yourself in such an intense way to doing something whose performance in money is small.

With Savings

Maybe you try to save and take crumbs from here and others from there, raking for your daily issues, and then maybe you could concentrate on that 20% of shares that would allow you to get 80% of your savings.

Personal Relationships

If you want to take care of your partner, 20% of your efforts produce 80% of the results. There are things that often go unnoticed but there are others that are valued. Thus, any detail in a complicated moment, such as an illness, the death of a family member, or a decline is valued much more than under normal circumstances.

In the same way, it is convenient that you do not forget that the same happens with errors. Think, for example, of forgetting something. Maybe it doesn't matter. But concern to you if you forget your girl's birthday. Perhaps there can also be many discussions without transcendence, but if the discussion is at the wedding of your partner's sister it may be much more serious than many others added together.

Our Colleagues

Possibly although it sounds bad to say it, 20% of our friends will produce 80% of the benefits of friendship. I do not defend you get rid of the remaining 80%, but maybe I defend that your attention need not be distributed equally among all.

Problems

20% of the problems produce 80% of the headaches. So when you want to solve problems, think about the effect that each of them has on your well-being and dedicate more time to the problems that may affect you the most. Maybe it's a problem that the garage door squeaks, but the potential consequences of anger with your boss are much more relevant.

Everyday Tasks

It has happened many times I have written in a list the things I have to do during the day and almost without realizing you end up treating all the things pointed as if they were similar in relevance. However, this is not the case. I can write on the same sheet on how to pay income tax and call a friend. And seeing everything together, I can have the feeling that if I call my friend, I have achieved 80% of the result when that is far from being true.

Tips To Improve Your Life

Every day, on different websites, in social networks, in the books you read, you discover rules that can interest to apply in your daily life. And possibly each of those rules has a part of the reason. But it is not possible to apply them all. So choose and think about what are the rules that will benefit you the most. The rules that will give you 80% of the result.

FOURTEEN

Why Is the Right Mindset So Important?

Do you feel uncomfortable in certain situations and call for more self-assertion? Does the prospect of presentations drive you to get beads of sweat on your forehead? Then maybe it's time to switch your mindset.

Our mindset is represented by so many memories and experiences that have long since arrived in the subconscious and even produce their sometimes braking effect. With the proper mindset, however, you will conquer old obstacles.

Change Mindset: How to Set Up For More Success

Success is a big weighty word. What is a success? And in what do you require to be successful? Everyone has to specify that for themselves. They are, for example:

Success at Work

Success in Relationships

Success in Sports Challenges

One fact is certain. Standstill is death. Successful people understand they need to grow and they like to do so, are open to fresh experiences. You can and should learn from such individuals to get a new mindset. Surround yourself with people who have experienced similar to yours but have overcome their traditional means of thinking.

Of course, particular traits, such as sensitivity to defeat or setbacks, can help us develop a specific mindset. But Dweck's researches with juveniles and students also determine that the mindset can be entirely developed and transformed through interactions.

And that positive thinking can help not merely reduce pressure but still contribute to health had long been identified in psychology.

Changing one's mindset is a process. You should start with the following tips:

Be Receptive To New Things

Take on new challenges and learn to handle the failures. Making mistakes is a part of life, setbacks too. Proverbs like "there is no master yet fallen from the sky." That's precisely what they say. If you wish to accomplish something, be engaged. This comprises not solely the enthusiasm to learn new things, but also to break new ground. If something does not work in one situation, it can nevertheless work in a different situation.

Be Patient

Many restrain themselves with negative beliefs by always repeating in their minds the old experiences or attributions. I cannot do that. I'm too clumsy or stupid. Put a stopper in front. Yet perhaps you cannot handle a specific task. But that does not mean it stays that way, but cheers you on. You would not even call out to a long-distance runner. That will never happen; the track is way too long or difficult and so on. The chances of doing something with the right attitude and self-love are much higher.do you accept the challenge

If you get assigned a task at work you find difficult and unfamiliar with, try it anyway. Although it is laborious, you will cope better with it next time. Try and you will make progress.

Stay Realistic

Do not become too much a perfectionist in your claims. There is always something you can improve. But you can follow the Pareto Principle. Train your skills and try to learn new ones.

Learn to Deal with Setbacks

As mentioned at the beginning, defeats belong to it. At another time, with a different method, with suggestions from colleagues, they can still accomplish tasks. Just because something does not work right away does not mean that you have failed. You may just have to choose a different approach. Tell yourself that you almost made it. But celebrate your achievements. Not just the big ones, but also the little ones. Step by step, work your way forward and duly acknowledge this.

Conclusion

Most books or tapes on personal success and achievement describe the value of goal setting as a central key to achieving success in any endeavor. You cannot go anywhere if you do not know where you desire to go.

Napoleon Hill outlined the significance of having a distinct purpose as one of the fundamental factors in achieving success. He stated it is the starting point of all accomplishments and that its absence is the stumbling block for ninety-eight out of every hundred individuals only because they never established their goals and move on them.

All great success individuals in each area of life whether be it an actor, athlete or writer will attest to having a clear goal. The challenge is that we've heard it so often that we fall off into the tap of familiarity. Unless you do it and practice it daily, you do not know it. You might know of it, but unless you do it, you do not know it.

With goals, you create the future in advance. With goals, you create your destiny. You need goals that inspire you. With strong goals, something drives you to grow and expand and develop yourselves towards what you want from and for your life. Compelling goals have the potential to move you. Done properly and precisely, goals can transform your life.

About the Author

Monique Joiner Siedlak is a writer, witch, and warrior on a mission to awaken people to their greatest potential through the power of storytelling infused with mysticism, modern paganism, and new age spirituality. At the young age of 12, she began rigorously studying the fascinating philosophy of Wicca. By the time she was 20, she was self-initiated into the craft, and hasn't looked back ever since. To this day, she has authored over 40 books pertaining to the magick and mysteries of life.

To find out more about Monique Joiner Siedlak artistically, spiritually, and personally, feel free to visit her **official website**.

www.mojosiedlak.com

facebook.com/mojosiedlak

twitter.com/mojosiedlak

instagram.com/mojosiedlak

pinterest.com/mojosiedlak

bookbub.com/authors/monique-joiner-siedlak

Practical Magick

Wiccan Basics

Candle Magick

Wiccan Spells

Love Spells

Abundance Spells

Herb Magick

Moon Magick

Creating Your Own Spells

Gypsy Magic

Protection Magick

African Magic

Hoodoo

Seven African Powers: The Orishas

Cooking For the Orishas

Lucumi: The Ways of Santeria

Voodoo of Louisiana

The Yoga Collective

Yoga for Beginners

Yoga for Stress

Yoga for Back Pain

Yoga for Weight Loss

Yoga for Flexibility

Yoga for Advanced Beginners

Yoga for Fitness

Yoga for Runners

Yoga for Energy

Yoga for Your Sex Life

Yoga to Beat Depression and Anxiety

Yoga for Menstruation

Yoga to Detox Your Body

Toga to Tone Your Body

A Natural Beautiful You

Creating Your Own Body Butter

Creating Your Own Body Scrub

Creating Your Own Body Spray

Last Chance
Join My Newsletter!

If you missed it, I have a free gift available for you and wanted to remind you it's still available.

mojosiedlak.com/self-help-and-yoga-newsletter

Thank you for reading my book.
I really appreciate all your feedback and would love to hear what you have to say!
Please leave your review at your favorite retailer!

www.ingramcontent.com/pod-product-compliance
Lightning Source LLC
Chambersburg PA
CBHW071631040426
42452CB00009B/1577